PICTURE LIBRARY

HURRICANES
AND
TORNADOES

OF BARRETT

PICTURE LIBRARY

HURRICANES
AND
TORNADOES

Norman Barrett

Franklin Watts

London   New York   Sydney   Toronto

© 1989 Franklin Watts

First published in Great Britain
  1989 by
Franklin Watts
98 Leonard Street
London EC2A 4RH

First published in the USA by
Franklin Watts Inc
387 Park Avenue South
New York
NY 10016

First published in Australia by
Franklin Watts
14 Mars Road
Lane Cove
NSW 2066

UK ISBN: 0 86313 881 0
US ISBN: 0-531-10837-6
Library of Congress Catalog Card
Number 89-31503

Printed in Italy

Designed by
Barrett & Weintroub

Photographs by
N.S. Barrett Collection
Blake Allison Jr
Colin Crane
Crown Copyright
Everyday Weather Project/State
  University of New York
Richard Fillhart
M.P. Garrod
Joseph H. Golden
Joseph Haines
NASA
National Center for
  Atmospheric Research/National
  Science Foundation
National Meteorological Library
NOAA
Roger Wakimoto

Illustration by
Peter Bull Art

Technical Consultant
Mary Spence

Contents

Introduction

Hurricanes and tornadoes are storms that can cause devastating damage in some parts of the world.

A hurricane is a whirling storm of violent wind and rain. It lasts for several hours, and may measure hundreds of kilometres across.

Tornadoes are twisting wind storms. They measure as much as a few hundred metres across and are the most violent winds on earth.

△ A tornado near Oklahoma City, in the United States. A tornado is a fearful sight as it reaches down from the clouds and twists its way viciously across the land.

Hurricanes form over the oceans in tropical regions. They grow and become stronger as they move. Their winds whirl round a calm area called the eye.

A tornado is a rotating cloud that funnels downwards from a mass of dark clouds. It does not always reach the earth. If it does, it destroys almost everything in its path. A tornado that occurs over water is called a waterspout.

△ A twisted mass of trees and metal is the result of a hurricane in Alabama, in the southern United States. Hurricane damage is often widespread, affecting areas spanning hundreds of kilometres.

Whirling winds

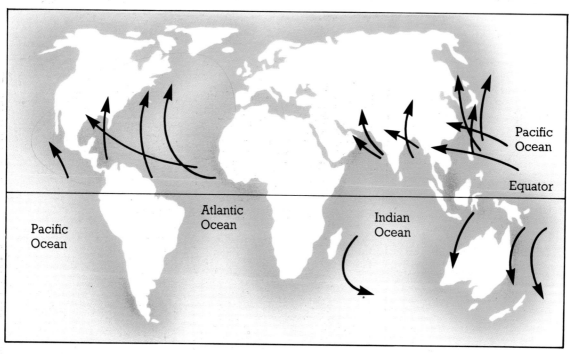

Pacific
Ocean

Equator

Atlantic
Ocean

Indian
Ocean

Pacific
Ocean

The arrows on the world map (above) show where hurricanes begin over the oceans and the typical paths they take. They are called typhoons or tropical cyclones in some parts of the world.

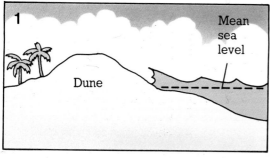

1

Mean
sea
level

Dune

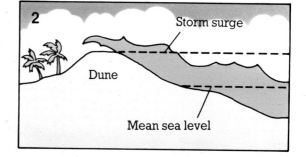

2

Storm surge

Dune

Mean sea level

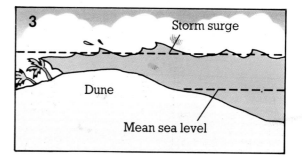

3

Storm surge

Dune

Mean sea level

Storm surge

All is peaceful on shore (1) before a hurricane strikes. As the hurricane approaches, the sea level rises and a storm surge builds up (2). The water flattens protective dunes and floods the land behind them (3).

The Beaufort Scale

The Beaufort Scale is a set of standard wind forces. Numbers from 1 to 12 represent the strength of the wind, from light air to hurricane. As the speed of the wind increases, its effect can be seen first on smoke, then on trees, and then by the damage it causes. The standard wind strengths are given in mph (1 mph = 1.6 km/h).

Light air 1-3 mph

Slight breeze 4-7 mph

Gentle breeze 8-12 mph

Moderate breeze 13-18 mph

Fresh breeze 19-24 mph

Strong breeze 25-31 mph

High wind 32-38 mph

Gale 39-46 mph

Strong gale 47-54 mph

Whole gale 55-63 mph

Storm 64-72 mph

Hurricane 73 mph or more

Life of a hurricane

Hurricanes begin in the warm oceans. The air above the ocean is warmed and rises. It takes up water from the ocean. Cool air rushes in to take its place, and this in turn warms, rises and picks up water.

As this process continues, it speeds up. The winds get faster and stronger and begin to swirl around. Huge thunderclouds build up. The whole system measures hundreds of kilometres across and rotates around the calm eye.

▽ A satellite picture shows what a hurricane looks like from above. It extends over an area spanning several hundred kilometres.

Hurricane winds blow round the eye in an anti-clockwise direction in the Northern Hemisphere. They blow clockwise in the Southern Hemisphere.

Most hurricanes blow westwards at first. Many die out over the ocean, but some turn in towards land. Before they blow themselves out, they may create havoc, especially on and near the coast.

△ A picture taken from the air shows the formation of a huge anvil-shaped thundercloud as a storm begins to grow.

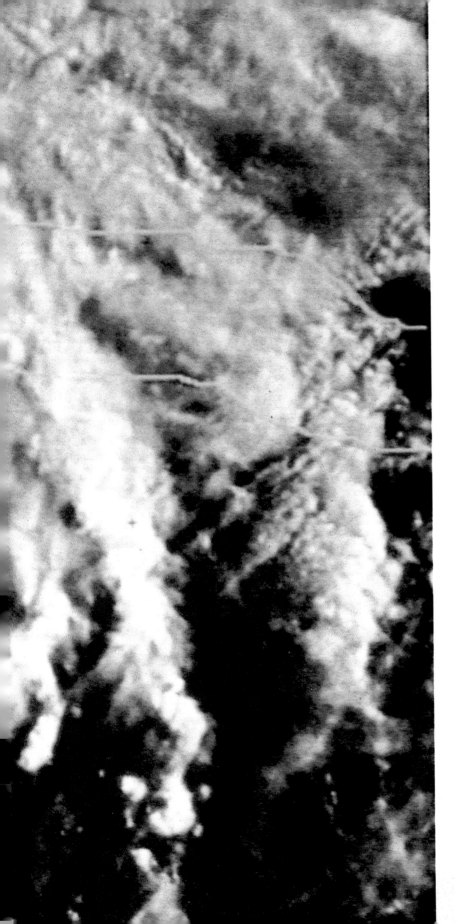

◁ A satellite picture taken from directly above a hurricane shows the eye clearly and the massive swirling clouds around it.

The hurricane is moving over the Caribbean, and the outline of western Cuba has been drawn in. The whole picture covers an east-west distance of about 800 km (500 miles).

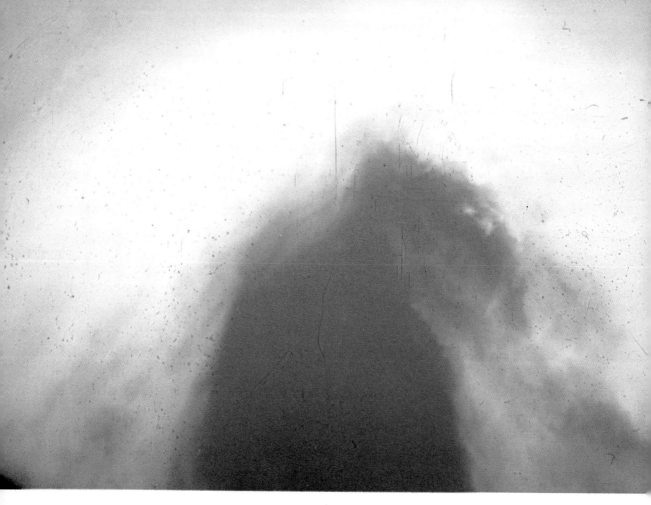

A hurricane's strongest winds and heaviest rains occur in the clouds that surround the eye. These are called wall clouds. Their winds may blow at speeds of up to 200 to 240 km/h (125 to 150 mph).

The eye itself has little wind or cloud. It moves, as does the hurricane as a whole, at speeds of between 15 and 50 km/h (10 and 30 mph).

△ Looking up inside the eye of a hurricane. An eye might measure 30 km (20 miles) across.

Devastation

A hurricane produces huge waves in the ocean called a storm surge. These waves rise several metres above the normal seas. As the hurricane comes ashore, the storm surge builds up and washes away coastal defences such as dunes, flooding the coastal area.

As the hurricane moves over land, fierce winds and heavy rain pound the area for several hours. There is a period of calm for nearly an hour as the eye passes over.

▽ The palms bend in the force of the wind, the skies darken and the sea waves build up as a hurricane comes ashore.

△ Widespread flooding in coastal areas is often the most devastating effect of a hurricane.

◁ Telegraph poles come crashing down as a hurricane moves across the land. It is not safe to be on the roads.

Getting caught in a hurricane is a frightening experience. The winds howl alarmingly and the rain lashes down with great ferocity.

Structures begin to strain and creak and come crashing down – trees, telegraph poles, even houses. Branches, slates and even whole roofs fly dangerously through the air. Cars and mobile homes are overturned and sometimes swept away by the flood waters.

▽ The hurricane damage here does not look too bad – no more than a bent lamp-post – until you notice that the mobile home has been flipped over completely!

Hurricane precautions

There is no way to stop a hurricane. But hurricanes can be spotted and tracked as they begin to form and move across the ocean. Weather forecasters are able to predict where they will strike land, and send out warnings.

The first hurricane precautions that need to be taken are usually at sea. People bring their boats in and moor them securely. Mobile homes on the coast are anchored to the ground with strong cables.

▽ Scientists called meteorologists study the weather. They use information from weather satellites in space, weather stations around the world and coastal radar to track and plot the path of hurricanes.

BEST TRACK
VASTRA FCST

HURRICANE ALICIA
AUG 16 1983 1200GMT

People who live in the predicted path of a hurricane secure their homes and move inland. If they cannot get away, they take other precautions. They stay indoors, away from windows. Windows can be taped to stop them from shattering.

After a severe hurricane, there may be no electricity, gas or water. It helps to have ready a portable gas supply for light and heat, a torch, a battery radio and a bath full of water.

△ Computers are used to help predict the path of a hurricane. Each hurricane is named from lists approved by the World Meteorological Organization. The first hurricane of the season is allotted a name beginning with A, the second with B and so on.

Tornadoes

Most tornadoes form at a boundary, or front, between a mass of cool dry air and a mass of warm humid air. A narrow band of storm clouds called a squall line develops at this front.

Sometimes the warm air rises rapidly and is replaced by more warm air. This rushes in and also rises. It may begin to rotate, forming a tornado.

Tornadoes are usually over in less than an hour, although some have been known to last several hours.

▷ A tornado in Western Australia. When a tornado's funnel reaches the ground it pulls up a huge cloud of dust.

▽ The devastation left after a tornado swept through Xenia, Ohio. Tornadoes occur in many parts of the world, but are most common in the United States, especially in the Midwestern and Southern states.

◁ A huge, dark tornado sweeps over Texas. Most tornadoes travel about 30 km (20 miles) at speeds of 15 to 40 km/h (10–25 mph). But some travel 10 times as far at speeds of up to 100 km/h (60 mph). The winds whirl round the centre of the storm at speeds as high as 500 km/h (300 mph). The destructive force of a tornado comes partly from its ability to suck up air. This creates great pressure differences between, say, the inside and outside of a house, causing it to explode.

▷ The three pictures on the right show stages in the development of a tornado over a period of nearly 15 minutes. Out of the dense, dark storm cloud (top) there develops a twisting funnel cloud, which can be seen raising dust from the ground (centre). The tornado continues on its way (bottom).

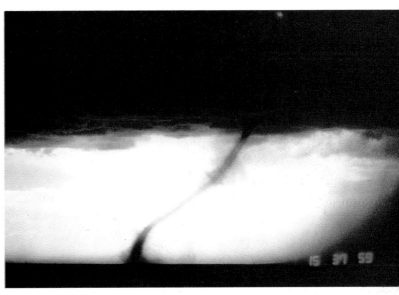

Waterspouts

When a tornado occurs over water, it is called a waterspout. But unlike tornadoes over land, which raise dust, waterspouts do not raise water. The funnel is a column of whirling air and watery mist.

The mist of a waterspout is formed by the rapid cooling of moist air as it rushes into the low pressure area at the centre of the column.

◁ A tornado moves menacingly towards an airport.

▽ A waterspout is a tornado over an ocean or lake.

△ A waterspout begins to develop.

◁ An aerial view of a waterspout as it approaches the Florida Keys, a chain of islands off the south-eastern coast of the United States.

▷ This ship might have to change course as a waterspout is spotted in the distance. The violent winds of a waterspout can seriously damage ships and capsize small boats.

The story of devastating winds

God of storms

The word hurricane comes from the Arawak language of the West Indies, where the god of storms was known as Huracan. The term is now also used for similar storms elsewhere in the world, such as the typhoons of the Northern Pacific Ocean and the cyclones of the Southern Pacific and Indian Ocean. In Australia, tropical cyclones are called "willy-willies".

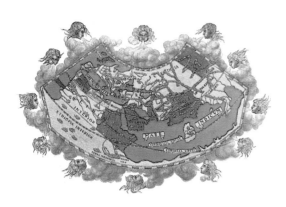

△ A world map originally drawn over 1,800 years ago depicts powerful winds blowing from every corner of the earth.

Strong winds

Seafarers of ancient times were very dependent on winds. In favourable winds, they could make good time. If there was no wind, they could be becalmed for weeks. But if they were caught in a typhoon or hurricane, their flimsy sailing vessels might be tossed around in the stormy seas and they would find it difficult to survive.

Storm disasters

Hurricanes and cyclones have caused some of the world's worst disasters. A cyclone originating in the Indian Ocean in 1970 caused an estimated one million deaths, mainly by flooding, in the Ganges Delta Islands of Bangladesh (then East Pakistan).

In the Western Hemisphere, hurricanes sweep in from the Atlantic about 10 times a year. The season usually lasts from May to September. Hurricanes cause extensive damage with considerable loss of life about once in every three years. In 1900, a hurricane and storm surge

△ A satellite view of the cyclone that caused one of the worst disasters ever, in Bangladesh in 1970.

caused about 6,000 deaths in the Galveston, Texas, area. In 1974, Hurricane Fifi was responsible for about 8,000 deaths in Honduras, in Central America.

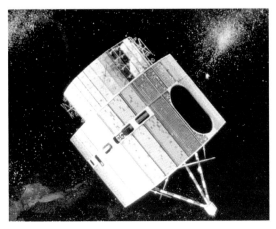

△ The development of weather satellites has resulted in earlier hurricane predictions.

Combating hurricanes

Scientists have tried to develop methods to prevent hurricanes reaching land. So far, however, experiments have met with little success.

Watches and warnings

The greatest defence against hurricanes has proved to be the weather satellite. Regular pictures taken from weather satellites orbiting the earth build up a picture of cloud movements. Any tropical storms detected are then carefully watched.

Weather aircraft may be sent up into the storms to gather more information. Meteorologists track the progress of storms and try to predict whether they will come ashore, and if so where. As a storm approaches land, it is picked up on coastal radar.

A "hurricane watch" is issued when there is a threat of hurricane conditions within 24 to 36 hours. A "warning" for a particular area is put out when hurricane conditions are predicted for 24 hours or less.

△ Special weather aircraft are sent into hurricanes to gather information about wind speed, rain and temperature.

Weather forecasting is not an exact science. But modern technology has made great advances in the prediction of hurricane behaviour. Thanks to the early warnings, many more lives are being saved every year.

Facts and records

Hailstones

Hailstones are often a product of hurricanes. The heaviest stones reported fell on Bangladesh in 1986, killing many people. Some weighed over 1 kg (2.2 lb).

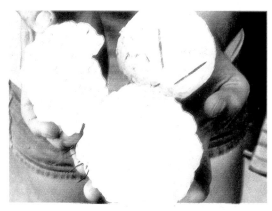

△ Hailstones sometimes reach huge sizes.

Storm surge

The highest storm surge recorded was one of 7.6 m (25 ft), which flooded the coast at Pass Christian, Mississippi, when Hurricane Camille came ashore in 1969. The hurricane killed more than 250 people in seven states, from Louisiana to Virginia.

Dust devils

Whirling columns of dust called "dust devils" occur in some parts of the world. They look like tornadoes, but are relatively harmless. They are caused by very strong local heating by the

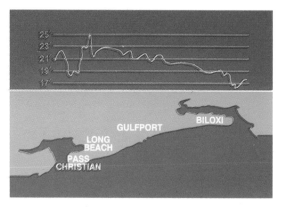

△ A record of the storm surge that hit the coast of Mississippi when Hurricane Camille struck.

sun in dry regions. Dust particles are swept round and round in a whirl no more than a few metres across, although they may rise to a height of 1,000 m (3,000 ft).

△ A dust devil in Kenya reaches high into the air.

Glossary

Beaufort Scale
A standard scale of wind strengths.

Cyclone
A term used for hurricane-type storms starting in the South Pacific or the Indian Ocean.

Eye
The calm centre of a hurricane

Front
The boundary where cold and warm air masses meet.

Funnel
The column of swirling air that reaches down from a tornado.

Humid
Humid air contains a high percentage of water vapour.

Hurricane warning
The warning put out when a hurricane is expected to strike within 24 hours.

Hurricane watch
A preliminary warning issued when there is a threat of a hurricane in the watch area.

Meteorologist
A scientist who studies the weather. Some meteorologists also do weather forecasting.

Radar
A method used for tracking movements in the air, of storms as well as aircraft.

Squall line
The narrow band of storm clouds that develops at a front when cold and warm air masses meet.

Storm surge
A great dome of water, often as much as 80 km (50 miles) wide, that sweeps across the coastline near where the eye of a hurricane comes ashore.

Typhoon
A term used for hurricane-type storms starting in the North Pacific Ocean.

Wall clouds
The clouds closest to the eye of a hurricane, with the strongest winds and heaviest rains.

Waterspout
A tornado that occurs over water.

Willy-willy
A term used in Australia for a tropical cyclone.

Index